# Color By Numbers Adult Coloring Book of

# Mermaids

## ZenMaster Coloring Books

# COLOR TEST PAGE

# COLOR TEST PAGE

1. Buttermilk
2. Sunglow
3. Lightning Yellow
4. Cadmium Orange
5. Scarlet Red
6. Dark Red
7. Ocean Rose
8. Purple Pink
9. Light Pink
10. Red Violet
11. Plum
12. Violet
13. Blue Violet
14. Blue Bay
15. Light Blue
16. Denim Blue
17. Ocean Blue
18. Turquoise
19. Dark Blue
20. Seaweed Green
21. Emerald
22. Light Green
23. Moss Green
24. Olive Green
25. Willow Green
26. Flesh
27. Brown Ochre
28. Dark Brown
29. Dark Gray
30. Warm Gray
31. Light Gray

1. Buttermilk
2. Sunglow
3. Lightning Yellow
4. Cadmium Orange
5. Scarlet Red
6. Dark Red
7. Ocean Rose
8. Purple Pink
9. Light Pink
10. Red Violet
11. Plum
12. Violet
13. Blue Violet
14. Blue Bay
15. Light Blue
16. Denim Blue
17. Ocean Blue
18. Turquoise
19. Dark Blue
20. Seaweed Green
21. Emerald
22. Light Green
23. Moss Green
24. Olive Green
25. Willow Green
26. Flesh
27. Brown Ochre
28. Dark Brown
29. Dark Gray
30. Warm Gray
31. Light Gray

1. Buttermilk
2. Sunglow
3. Lightning Yellow
4. Cadmium Orange
5. Scarlet Red
6. Dark Red
7. Ocean Rose
8. Purple Pink
9. Light Pink
10. Red Violet
11. Plum
12. Violet
13. Blue Violet
14. Blue Bay
15. Light Blue
16. Denim Blue
17. Ocean Blue
18. Turquoise
19. Dark Blue
20. Seaweed Green
21. Emerald
22. Light Green
23. Moss Green
24. Olive Green
25. Willow Green
26. Flesh
27. Brown Ochre
28. Dark Brown
29. Dark Gray
30. Warm Gray
31. Light Gray

1. Buttermilk
2. Sunglow
3. Lightning Yellow
4. Cadmium Orange
5. Scarlet Red
6. Dark Red
7. Ocean Rose
8. Purple Pink
9. Light Pink
10. Red Violet
11. Plum
12. Violet
13. Blue Violet
14. Blue Bay
15. Light Blue
16. Denim Blue
17. Ocean Blue
18. Turquoise
19. Dark Blue
20. Seaweed Green
21. Emerald
22. Light Green
23. Moss Green
24. Olive Green
25. Willow Green
26. Flesh
27. Brown Ochre
28. Dark Brown
29. Dark Gray
30. Warm Gray
31. Light Gray

1. Buttermilk
2. Sunglow
3. Lightning Yellow
4. Cadmium Orange
5. Scarlet Red
6. Dark Red
7. Ocean Rose
8. Purple Pink
9. Light Pink
10. Red Violet
11. Plum
12. Violet
13. Blue Violet
14. Blue Bay
15. Light Blue
16. Denim Blue
17. Ocean Blue
18. Turquoise
19. Dark Blue
20. Seaweed Green
21. Emerald
22. Light Green
23. Moss Green
24. Olive Green
25. Willow Green
26. Flesh
27. Brown Ochre
28. Dark Brown
29. Dark Gray
30. Warm Gray
31. Light Gray

1. Buttermilk
2. Sunglow
3. Lightning Yellow
4. Cadmium Orange
5. Scarlet Red
6. Dark Red
7. Ocean Rose
8. Purple Pink
9. Light Pink
10. Red Violet
11. Plum
12. Violet
13. Blue Violet
14. Blue Bay
15. Light Blue
16. Denim Blue
17. Ocean Blue
18. Turquoise
19. Dark Blue
20. Seaweed Green
21. Emerald
22. Light Green
23. Moss Green
24. Olive Green
25. Willow Green
26. Flesh
27. Brown Ochre
28. Dark Brown
29. Dark Gray
30. Warm Gray
31. Light Gray

1. Buttermilk
2. Sunglow
3. Lightning Yellow
4. Cadmium Orange
5. Scarlet Red
6. Dark Red
7. Ocean Rose
8. Purple Pink
9. Light Pink
10. Red Violet
11. Plum
12. Violet
13. Blue Violet
14. Blue Bay
15. Light Blue
16. Denim Blue
17. Ocean Blue
18. Turquoise
19. Dark Blue
20. Seaweed Green
21. Emerald
22. Light Green
23. Moss Green
24. Olive Green
25. Willow Green
26. Flesh
27. Brown Ochre
28. Dark Brown
29. Dark Gray
30. Warm Gray
31. Light Gray

1. Buttermilk
2. Sunglow
3. Lightning Yellow
4. Cadmium Orange
5. Scarlet Red
6. Dark Red
7. Ocean Rose
8. Purple Pink
9. Light Pink
10. Red Violet
11. Plum
12. Violet
13. Blue Violet
14. Blue Bay
15. Light Blue
16. Denim Blue
17. Ocean Blue
18. Turquoise
19. Dark Blue
20. Seaweed Green
21. Emerald
22. Light Green
23. Moss Green
24. Olive Green
25. Willow Green
26. Flesh
27. Brown Ochre
28. Dark Brown
29. Dark Gray
30. Warm Gray
31. Light Gray

1. Buttermilk
2. Sunglow
3. Lightning Yellow
4. Cadmium Orange
5. Scarlet Red
6. Dark Red
7. Ocean Rose
8. Purple Pink
9. Light Pink
10. Red Violet
11. Plum
12. Violet
13. Blue Violet
14. Blue Bay
15. Light Blue
16. Denim Blue
17. Ocean Blue
18. Turquoise
19. Dark Blue
20. Seaweed Green
21. Emerald
22. Light Green
23. Moss Green
24. Olive Green
25. Willow Green
26. Flesh
27. Brown Ochre
28. Dark Brown
29. Dark Gray
30. Warm Gray
31. Light Gray

1. Buttermilk
2. Sunglow
3. Lightning Yellow
4. Cadmium Orange
5. Scarlet Red
6. Dark Red
7. Ocean Rose
8. Purple Pink
9. Light Pink
10. Red Violet
11. Plum
12. Violet
13. Blue Violet
14. Blue Bay
15. Light Blue
16. Denim Blue
17. Ocean Blue
18. Turquoise
19. Dark Blue
20. Seaweed Green
21. Emerald
22. Light Green
23. Moss Green
24. Olive Green
25. Willow Green
26. Flesh
27. Brown Ochre
28. Dark Brown
29. Dark Gray
30. Warm Gray
31. Light Gray

1. Buttermilk
2. Sunglow
3. Lightning Yellow
4. Cadmium Orange
5. Scarlet Red
6. Dark Red
7. Ocean Rose
8. Purple Pink
9. Light Pink
10. Red Violet
11. Plum
12. Violet
13. Blue Violet
14. Blue Bay
15. Light Blue
16. Denim Blue
17. Ocean Blue
18. Turquoise
19. Dark Blue
20. Seaweed Green
21. Emerald
22. Light Green
23. Moss Green
24. Olive Green
25. Willow Green
26. Flesh
27. Brown Ochre
28. Dark Brown
29. Dark Gray
30. Warm Gray
31. Light Gray

1. Buttermilk
2. Sunglow
3. Lightning Yellow
4. Cadmium Orange
5. Scarlet Red
6. Dark Red
7. Ocean Rose
8. Purple Pink
9. Light Pink
10. Red Violet
11. Plum
12. Violet
13. Blue Violet
14. Blue Bay
15. Light Blue
16. Denim Blue
17. Ocean Blue
18. Turquoise
19. Dark Blue
20. Seaweed Green
21. Emerald
22. Light Green
23. Moss Green
24. Olive Green
25. Willow Green
26. Flesh
27. Brown Ochre
28. Dark Brown
29. Dark Gray
30. Warm Gray
31. Light Gray

1. Buttermilk
2. Sunglow
3. Lightning Yellow
4. Cadmium Orange
5. Scarlet Red
6. Dark Red
7. Ocean Rose
8. Purple Pink
9. Light Pink
10. Red Violet
11. Plum
12. Violet
13. Blue Violet
14. Blue Bay
15. Light Blue
16. Denim Blue
17. Ocean Blue
18. Turquoise
19. Dark Blue
20. Seaweed Green
21. Emerald
22. Light Green
23. Moss Green
24. Olive Green
25. Willow Green
26. Flesh
27. Brown Ochre
28. Dark Brown
29. Dark Gray
30. Warm Gray
31. Light Gray

1. Buttermilk
2. Sunglow
3. Lightning Yellow
4. Cadmium Orange
5. Scarlet Red
6. Dark Red
7. Ocean Rose
8. Purple Pink
9. Light Pink
10. Red Violet
11. Plum
12. Violet
13. Blue Violet
14. Blue Bay
15. Light Blue
16. Denim Blue
17. Ocean Blue
18. Turquoise
19. Dark Blue
20. Seaweed Green
21. Emerald
22. Light Green
23. Moss Green
24. Olive Green
25. Willow Green
26. Flesh
27. Brown Ochre
28. Dark Brown
29. Dark Gray
30. Warm Gray
31. Light Gray

1. Buttermilk
2. Sunglow
3. Lightning Yellow
4. Cadmium Orange
5. Scarlet Red
6. Dark Red
7. Ocean Rose
8. Purple Pink
9. Light Pink
10. Red Violet
11. Plum
12. Violet
13. Blue Violet
14. Blue Bay
15. Light Blue
16. Denim Blue
17. Ocean Blue
18. Turquoise
19. Dark Blue
20. Seaweed Green
21. Emerald
22. Light Green
23. Moss Green
24. Olive Green
25. Willow Green
26. Flesh
27. Brown Ochre
28. Dark Brown
29. Dark Gray
30. Warm Gray
31. Light Gray

1. Buttermilk
2. Sunglow
3. Lightning Yellow
4. Cadmium Orange
5. Scarlet Red
6. Dark Red
7. Ocean Rose
8. Purple Pink
9. Light Pink
10. Red Violet
11. Plum
12. Violet
13. Blue Violet
14. Blue Bay
15. Light Blue
16. Denim Blue
17. Ocean Blue
18. Turquoise
19. Dark Blue
20. Seaweed Green
21. Emerald
22. Light Green
23. Moss Green
24. Olive Green
25. Willow Green
26. Flesh
27. Brown Ochre
28. Dark Brown
29. Dark Gray
30. Warm Gray
31. Light Gray

1. Buttermilk
2. Sunglow
3. Lightning Yellow
4. Cadmium Orange
5. Scarlet Red
6. Dark Red
7. Ocean Rose
8. Purple Pink
9. Light Pink
10. Red Violet
11. Plum
12. Violet
13. Blue Violet
14. Blue Bay
15. Light Blue
16. Denim Blue
17. Ocean Blue
18. Turquoise
19. Dark Blue
20. Seaweed Green
21. Emerald
22. Light Green
23. Moss Green
24. Olive Green
25. Willow Green
26. Flesh
27. Brown Ochre
28. Dark Brown
29. Dark Gray
30. Warm Gray
31. Light Gray

1. Buttermilk
2. Sunglow
3. Lightning Yellow
4. Cadmium Orange
5. Scarlet Red
6. Dark Red
7. Ocean Rose
8. Purple Pink
9. Light Pink
10. Red Violet
11. Plum
12. Violet
13. Blue Violet
14. Blue Bay
15. Light Blue
16. Denim Blue
17. Ocean Blue
18. Turquoise
19. Dark Blue
20. Seaweed Green
21. Emerald
22. Light Green
23. Moss Green
24. Olive Green
25. Willow Green
26. Flesh
27. Brown Ochre
28. Dark Brown
29. Dark Gray
30. Warm Gray
31. Light Gray

1. Buttermilk
2. Sunglow
3. Lightning Yellow
4. Cadmium Orange
5. Scarlet Red
6. Dark Red
7. Ocean Rose
8. Purple Pink
9. Light Pink
10. Red Violet
11. Plum
12. Violet
13. Blue Violet
14. Blue Bay
15. Light Blue
16. Denim Blue
17. Ocean Blue
18. Turquoise
19. Dark Blue
20. Seaweed Green
21. Emerald
22. Light Green
23. Moss Green
24. Olive Green
25. Willow Green
26. Flesh
27. Brown Ochre
28. Dark Brown
29. Dark Gray
30. Warm Gray
31. Light Gray

1. Buttermilk
2. Sunglow
3. Lightning Yellow
4. Cadmium Orange
5. Scarlet Red
6. Dark Red
7. Ocean Rose
8. Purple Pink
9. Light Pink
10. Red Violet
11. Plum
12. Violet
13. Blue Violet
14. Blue Bay
15. Light Blue
16. Denim Blue
17. Ocean Blue
18. Turquoise
19. Dark Blue
20. Seaweed Green
21. Emerald
22. Light Green
23. Moss Green
24. Olive Green
25. Willow Green
26. Flesh
27. Brown Ochre
28. Dark Brown
29. Dark Gray
30. Warm Gray
31. Light Gray

Thank you for supporting
ZenMaster Coloring Books

Your support means the world to us,
and we're thrilled to have you embark on this
creative journey with us.

Our small company strives to make a
BIG difference by helping those
who may be less fortunate.

This is why we proudly hire struggling
artists from around the world!

Our goal is to provide financial support to artists and
their families by enabling them to pursue their passions
and share their hard work and limitless talent with you!

Help support our hard working artists
by leaving a positive review on Amazon!

And follow us on Facebook for updates and
FREE COLORING PAGES!
https://www.facebook.com/zenmastercoloringbooks/

Check out more of our books at:
amazon.com/author/zenmastercoloringbooks

# Free Bonus Page!
## from:

## Large Print Simple and Easy
# Mandalas

https://www.amazon.com/dp/198151290x


# Also available in color by numbers!!
https://amzn.com/dp/198207616x

# Free Bonus Page!
## from:

## Large Print Adult Coloring Book of
# Kittens and Cats

https://www.amazon.com/dp/1983684775

## Also available in color by numbers!!
https://www.amazon.com/dp/1983687626

## And 5x8" Travel Size
https://www.amazon.com/dp/1727552121

# Free Bonus Page!
## from:

# Butterflies and Gardens
### Large Pring Coloring Book for Adults

https://www.amazon.com/dp/1977882978

## Also available in color by numbers!!
https://www.amazon.com/dp/1977932398

# Free Bonus Page!
## from:

## Large Print Adult Coloring Book of
# Dachshunds

https://www.amazon.com/dp/1977508456

## Also available in color by numbers!!

https://www.amazon.com/dp/1977842658

## And 5x8" Travel Size

https://www.amazon.com/dp/1977576079

# Free Bonus Page!
## from:

## Large Print Adult Coloring Book of
# Spring

https://www.amazon.com/dp/1985347024

## Also available in color by numbers!!
https://www.amazon.com/dp/1985375540

## And 5x8" Travel Size
https://www.amazon.com/dp/1726193357

# Free Bonus Page!
## from:

### Adult Coloring Book of
# Sweets and Treats

https://www.amazon.com/dp/1795668881

## Also available in color by numbers!!
https://www.amazon.com/dp/1795670983

## And 5x8" Travel Size
https://www.amazon.com/dp/1796511447

# Free Bonus Page!
## from:

## Zen Coloring Notebook

https://www.amazon.com/dp/1535457015

## Available in 9 different colors!

## Also available in 5x8" journal size

https://www.amazon.com/dp/1535540591